MAPPING WORKBOOK

KARL BYRAND

UNIVERSITY OF WISCONSIN – SHEBOYGAN

WORLD REGIONAL GEOGRAPHY

NINTH EDITION

PEARSON
Prentice
Hall

Upper Saddle River, NJ 07458

Editor-in-Chief, Science: Dan Kaveney
Acquisitions Editor: Jeff Howard
Associate Editor: Amanda Brown
Executive Managing Editor: Kathleen Schiaparelli
Senior Managing Editor: Nicole M. Jackson
Assistant Managing Editor: Karen Bosch Petrov
Production Editor: Traci Douglas
Supplement Cover Manager: Paul Gourhan
Supplement Cover Designer: Christopher Kossa
Manufacturing Buyer: Ilene Kahn
Manufacturing Manager: Alexis Heydt-Long

© 2007 Pearson Education, Inc.
Pearson Prentice Hall
Pearson Education, Inc.
Upper Saddle River, NJ 07458

Printed in the United States of America

10 9 8 7 6 5 4 3 2 1

ISBN 0-13-154775-5

Pearson Education Ltd., *London*
Pearson Education Australia Pty. Ltd., *Sydney*
Pearson Education Singapore, Pte. Ltd.
Pearson Education North Asia Ltd., *Hong Kong*
Pearson Education Canada, Inc., *Toronto*
Pearson Educación de Mexico, S.A. de C.V.
Pearson Education—Japan, *Tokyo*
Pearson Education Malaysia, Pte. Ltd.

Preface

To the instructor and the students:

This mapping workbook is designed to foster geographic literacy. The nine parts of the mapping workbook contain place name lists that are chiefly drawn from the regional maps contained at the beginning of each unit in the *World Regional Geography, 9/e* by Clawson/Johnson. These lists allow students to become better acquainted with the place names and physical features of the world's regions.

Unlike other mapping workbooks, this one also contains a series of conceptual exercises that go along with *World Regional Geography, 9/e*. For each unit in the text, there are two exercises that draw largely on material contained in the figures and tables. These conceptual exercises go beyond the mere labeling of place names and physical features on maps, but rather ask the student to examine map and table material to determine patterns and connections between geographic phenomena and then generally explain the processes responsible for these patterns and connections. It is hoped that through these types of exercises students will gain a greater understanding of the field of geography and the spatial interconnections between the regions of the world.

The material contained in the mapping workbook may be used as supplemental assignments for instructors teaching world regional geography courses. The maps and the exercises are formatted so that they can be individually removed from the workbook and handed in to the instructor.

Contents

Map Identification and Exercises for Part 1: Basic Concepts and Ideas

Identify the following features on workbook Map 1.1

Identify and label the following regions on Map 1.1

- Africa South of the Sahara
- Antarctica
- Asia
- Australia New Zealand and the Pacific Islands
- Europe

- Latin America
- Russia and Central Eurasia
- The Middle East and North Africa
- United States and Canada

Identify and label the following features on Map 1.1

- Arctic Ocean
- Atlantic Ocean
- Indian Ocean
- Pacific Ocean
- Antarctic Circle
- Caribbean Sea
- North Sea
- Baltic Sea
- Mediterranean Sea
- Black Sea

- Arctic Circle
- Equator
- Prime Meridian
- Tropic of Cancer
- Tropic of Capricorn

Map 1.1

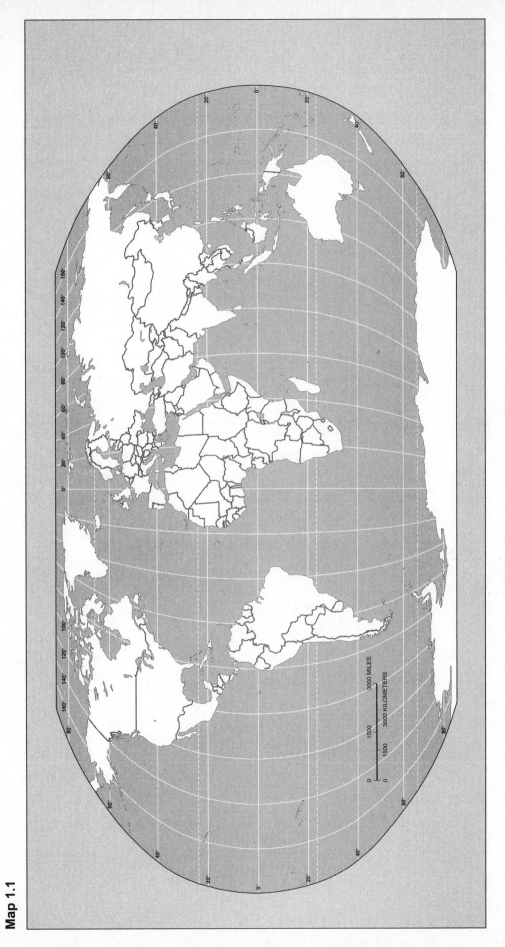

More Developed and Less Developed Regions of the World

Using the blank world map in your mapping workbook and Figure 3-20, World per-capita GNI PPP, (pages 72-73); Figure 3-26, World per-capita consumption of inanimate energy, expressed in oil equivalents (pages 80-81); Figure 3-27, World life expectancy at birth (pages 82-83); and the blank map provided (workbook Map 1.2), please complete the below exercise and answer the following questions.

1. Briefly study Figure 3-20 (World per-capita GNI PPP, pp. 72-73) taking note of national and regional differences in GNI PPP. Based on your observations from this data draw a line, or a series of lines, on Map 1.2 delineating what you would consider to be more developed and less developed countries and/or regions.

2. Do the same as above with Figure 3-26 (World per-capita consumption of inanimate energy expressed in oil equivalents pp. 80-81). Study this map in your text and make note of national and regional differences in energy consumption. Using a different colored pen, pencil, or marker, delineate more and less developed countries and/or regions on Map 1.2 based on per-capita energy consumption.

3. Study Figure 3-27 (World life expectancy at birth, pp. 82-83). Using a different colored pen, pencil, or marker do the same as the above, but this time using the data from life expectancy at birth as the trait to determine more and less developed countries/regions.

Once you have performed the above steps, study the development map you have created and answer the following questions:

1. According to your observations of the data and the map you have generated from it, where are the major more developed and less developed countries of the world?

   _____

   _____

   _____

   _____

   _____

2. Based on your map, where are the regions that reveal the greatest correlation between the three variables (i.e., life expectancy, GNI PPP, and energy consumption)?

   _____

   _____

   _____

   _____

   _____

3. Are there any countries or regions that display little to no correlation (i.e., outliers) with two of the other variables? If so, what factors may account for this?

   _____

   _____

   _____

   _____

   _____

4. If a country does not possess two or three of the variables you have mapped, do you believe that it should still be considered a more developed or less developed nation?

_____

_____

_____

_____

_____

5. Compare your map with Figure 3-29 (More developed and less developed regions of the world, pp. 86-87). Are there major differences between your map of more and less developed nations and Figure 3-29? For example, what areas have you delineated as more developed or less developed that Figure 3-29 may not have? What do you think may account for the discrepancies found?

_____

_____

_____

_____

_____

Map 1.2

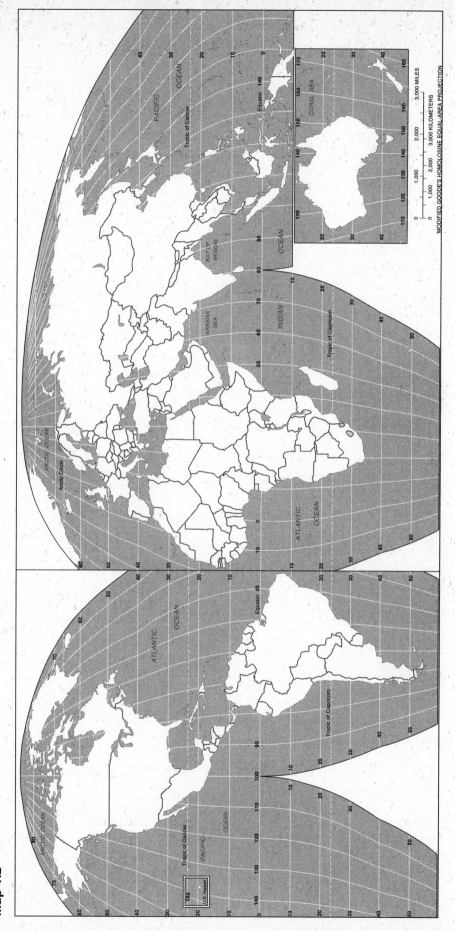

MODIFIED GOODE'S HOMOLOSINE EQUAL-AREA PROJECTION

Demographic Transition Map of the World

Go to page 30 of your textbook, read the section on *Models and Theories of Population Change*, and study Figure 2-9, Model of demographic transformation. After you do that, briefly study Figure 2-10, World population growth rates on page 32 and 33. Using the blank world map provided (workbook Map 1.3) do the following:

1. Label slow growth countries with a #4.
2. Label moderate growth countries with a #3.
3. Label rapid and very rapid growth countries with a #2.

Once you have created your map, answer the following questions.

1. Do you notice specific patterns of countries in regard to their stage in the demographic transformation? (i.e., does there appear to be a clustering of countries in stages two, three, or four?)

   _____

   _____

   _____

   _____

   _____

2. How can you explain the patterns that are exhibited? What do you believe to be the primary causes for these patterns?

   _____

   _____

   _____

   _____

   _____

3. Are there any countries that appear to be outliers in the demographic transformation patterns? (i.e., stage three or four countries surrounded by stage two countries)

   _____

   _____

   _____

   _____

   _____

4. How can you explain the patterns of the outliers that you may have observed?

   _____

   _____

   _____

   _____

   _____

Map 1.3

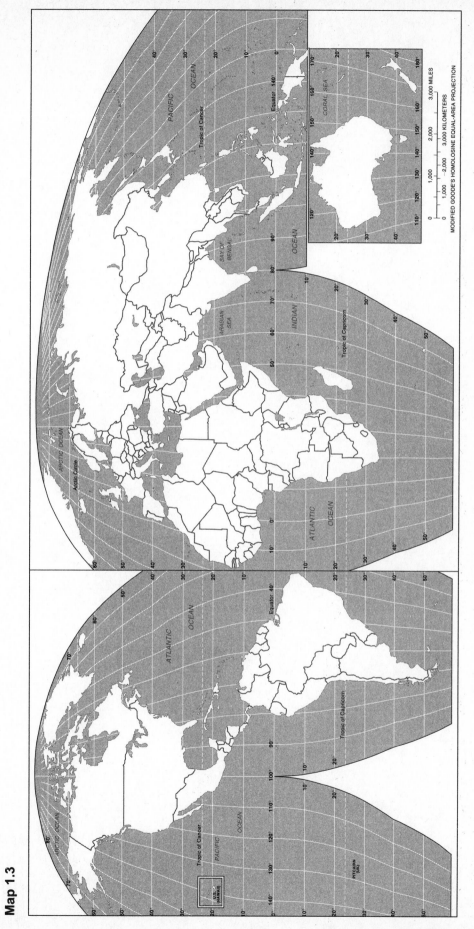

MODIFIED GOODE'S HOMOLOSINE EQUAL-AREA PROJECTION

Map Identification and Exercises for Part 2: United States and Canada

Identify the following features on workbook Maps 2.1 and 2.2

Identify and label the following countries on Map 2.1

- Canada
- United States

Identify and label the following states and provinces on Map 2.1

- Alberta
- British Columbia
- Manitoba
- New Brunswick
- Newfoundland
- Northwest Territory
- Nova Scotia
- Nunavut
- Ontario
- Prince Edward Island
- Quebec
- Saskatchewan
- Yukon
- Alabama
- Alaska
- Arizona
- Arkansas
- California
- Colorado
- Connecticut
- Delaware
- District of Columbia
- Florida
- Georgia
- Hawaii
- Idaho
- Illinois
- Indiana
- Iowa
- Kansas
- Kentucky
- Louisiana

- Maine
- Maryland
- Massachusetts
- Michigan
- Minnesota
- Mississippi
- Missouri
- Montana
- Nebraska
- Nevada
- New Hampshire
- New Jersey
- New Mexico
- New York
- North Carolina
- North Dakota
- Ohio
- Oklahoma
- Oregon
- Pennsylvania
- Rhode Island
- South Carolina
- South Dakota
- Tennessee
- Texas
- Utah
- Vermont
- Virginia
- Washington
- West Virginia
- Wisconsin
- Wyoming

Identify and label the following cities on Map 2.2

- Albuquerque
- Anchorage
- Atlanta
- Baltimore
- Birmingham
- Boston
- Buffalo
- Calgary
- Charlotte
- Charlottetown

- Cincinnati
- Cleveland
- Denver
- Detroit
- Edmonton
- Halifax
- Hartford
- Honolulu
- Houston
- Juneau

- Kansas City
- Las Vegas
- Los Angeles
- Memphis
- Miami
- Milwaukee
- Minneapolis-St. Paul
- Montreal
- Nashville
- New Orleans
- New York City
- Ottawa
- Philadelphia
- Phoenix
- Portland
- Providence
- Regina
- Richmond
- Salt Lake City
- San Antonio
- San Francisco
- Seattle
- St. John
- St. John's
- St. Louis
- Toronto
- Vancouver
- Winnipeg
- Yellowknife

Identify and label the following physical features on Map 2.2

- Alaska Range
- Appalachian Mountains
- Baffin Island
- Brooks Range
- Cape Breton Island
- Cascade Range
- Coast Mountains
- Coast Ranges
- Colorado Plateau
- Florida Keys
- Great Plains
- Island of Newfoundland
- Rocky Mountains
- Sierra Nevada Range
- Arctic Ocean
- Athabasca River
- Atlantic Ocean
- Baffin Bay
- Columbia River
- Fraser River
- Gulf of Mexico
- Hudson Bay
- Mackenzie River
- Mississippi River
- Missouri River
- Ohio River
- Pacific Ocean
- Peace River
- Rio Grande River
- Slave River
- St. Lawrence River
- Yukon River

Map 2.1

Map 2.2

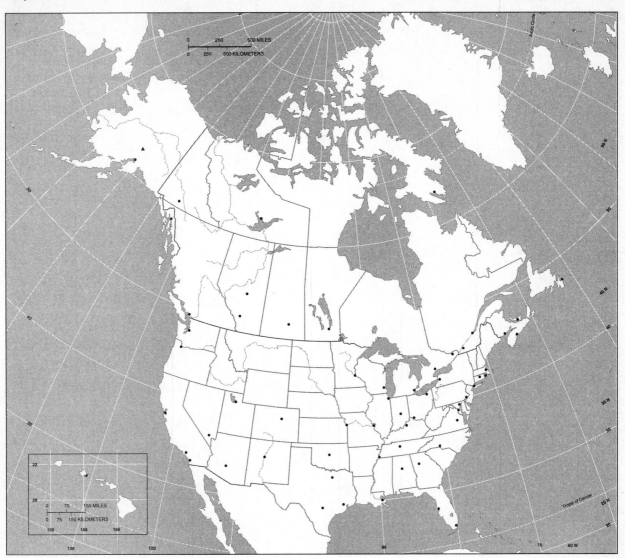

Patterns of Race and Ethnicity in the United States

Complete the following exercise, using Figure 6-4, African-American population as a percentage of county population in the United States in 2000 (page 155); Figure 6-6, Hispanic American population as a percentage of county population in the United States in 2000 (page 159); Figure 6-9, Native American population as a percentage of county population in the United States in 2000 (page 161); Figure 6-11, Asian American population as a percentage of county population in the United States in 2000 (page 164); and the blank map provided (workbook Map 2.3).

1. Using Figure 6-4 (page 155), find the U.S. region with the greatest concentration of African Americans. On the blank map provided, circle and shade in the region that would have the largest percentage of African Americans.
2. Using different colored pencils, do the same as above for the Hispanic American population (Figure 6-6, on page 159), the Native American population (Figure 6-9, on page 161), and the Asian American population (Figure 6-11, on page 164).

Once you have done this, study the map you have created and answer the following questions.

1. Where are the predominant regions of African American, Hispanic American, Native American, and Asian American concentration?

_____

_____

_____

_____

_____

2. What do you think accounts for the displayed patterns?

_____

_____

_____

_____

3. Do you notice any significant overlap among these minority populations in the United States? Why or why not?

_____

_____

_____

_____

_____

4. Where are the U.S. regions that seem to possess few of these minorities? How do you think that these patterns can be explained?

_____

_____

_____

_____

_____

_____

_____

_____

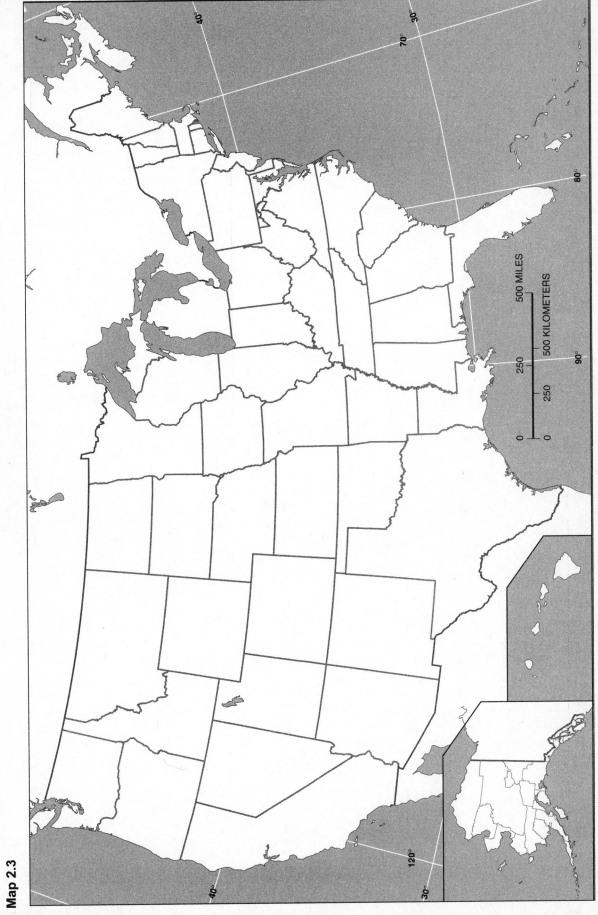

Map 2.3

500 MILES

500 KILOMETERS

250

250

0

0

Mapping Regions of Orographic Precipitation in the United States

Go to page 108 of your textbook and read the Geography in Action box *Landforms and Climate: Orographic Effects in the United States*. After reading this, go to Figure 4-1, Land surface regions of the United States and Canada (page 98), and study the location of the major North American mountain ranges. Using the blank North American map provided (workbook Map 2.4), do the following:

1. Draw a line designating the mountain ranges that would receive orographic precipitation.
2. Draw arrows representing the direction of what you would believe to be the prevailing winds in North America.
3. Shade in the areas along these mountain ranges that would be on the windward side.
4. Shade in the areas of these mountain ranges that would be on the leeward side.

Once you have completed the above, study the map you have created and answer the following questions.

1. Which areas would receive the greatest amounts of orographic precipitation?

_____
_____
_____
_____
_____
_____

2. Which areas would be in the rain shadow?

_____
_____
_____
_____
_____
_____

3. How would these precipitation patterns have an effect on the climates in these mountain regions?

_____
_____
_____
_____
_____
_____

Review Figure 4-10 Climate Regions in the United States and Canada on page 106 and answer question #4.

4. Does the climate map confirm your assumptions as to where the greatest and least amounts of precipitation would occur? Were there any discrepancies between your map and Figure 4-10?

_____

_____

_____

_____

_____

_____

_____

_____

_____

Map 2.4

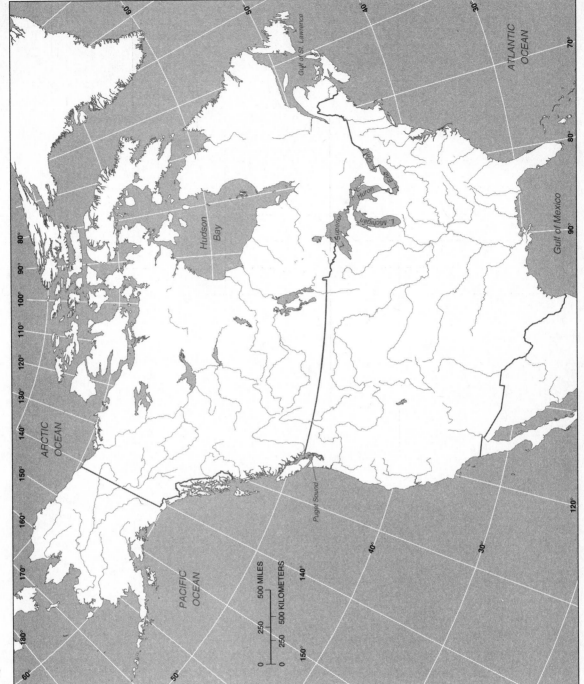

ATLANTIC OCEAN

Gulf of St. Lawrence

Gulf of Mexico

Hudson Bay

L. Michigan

Huron

Superior

ARCTIC OCEAN

Puget Sound

PACIFIC OCEAN

500 MILES

500 KILOMETERS

250

250

0

0

80°

90°

100°

110°

120°

130°

140°

150°

160°

170°

180°

60°

50°

40°

30°

120°

140°

150°

30°

40°

50°

60°

70°

80°

90°

Map Identification and Exercises for Part 3: Latin America and the Caribbean

Identify the following features on workbook Maps 3.1 and 3.2

Identify and label the following countries on Map 3.1

- Anguilla
- Antigua and Barbuda
- Argentina
- Bahamas
- Barbados
- Belize
- Bolivia
- Brazil
- Chile
- Columbia
- Costa Rica
- Cuba
- Dominica
- Dominican Republic
- Ecuador
- El Salvador
- French Guiana
- Grenada
- Guatemala
- Guyana
- Haiti
- Honduras
- Jamaica
- Martinique
- Mexico
- Nicaragua
- Panama
- Paraguay
- Peru
- Puerto Rico
- St. Kitts and Nevis
- St. Lucia
- St. Vincent and the Grenadines
- Suriname
- Trinidad and Tobago
- Uruguay
- Venezuela

Identify and label the following cities on Map 3.2

- Asuncion
- Belmopan
- Bogotá
- Brasilia
- Bridgetown
- Buenos Aries
- Caracas
- Cayenne
- Cuidad Juarez
- Georgetown
- Guatemala City
- Havana
- Iquitos
- Kingston
- La Paz
- Lima
- Managua
- Mexico City
- Monterrey
- Montevideo
- Nassau
- Panama
- Paramaribo
- Port of Spain
- Port-au-Prince
- Quito
- Rio de Janeiro
- Roseau
- San Jose
- San Juan
- San Salvador
- Santiago
- Santo Domingo
- St. George's
- St. John's
- Sucre
- Tegucigalpa

Identify and label the following physical features on Map 3.2

- Andes Mountains
- Cordillera Occidental
- Cordillera Oriental
- Serra Da Mantiqueira
- Serra Do Mar
- Sierra Madre Oriental
- Amazon Basin
- Falkland Islands
- Galapagos Islands
- Greater Antilles

- Sierra Madre Del Sur
- Sierra Madre Occidental
- Mato Grosso Plateau
- Pampas
- Parana Basalt Plateau
- Yucatan Peninsula
- Amazon River
- Atlantic Ocean

- Lesser Antilles
- Llanos
- Caribbean Sea
- Negro River
- Orinoco River
- Pacific Ocean
- Parana River
- Uruguay River

Map 3.1

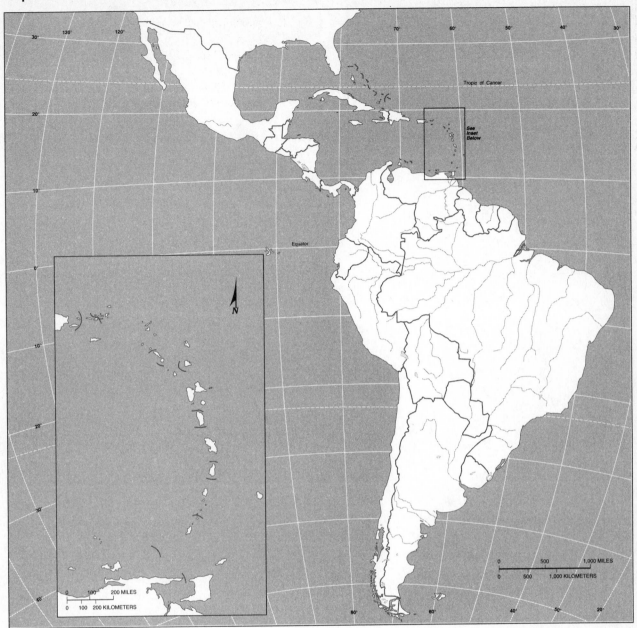

Map 3.2

Changing Dominant Cultures in the Caribbean

Using Table 8-1, The Caribbean Culture Realm in 2005, on page 212 of your textbook and the blank maps provided (workbook Maps 3.3 and 3.4), complete the following exercise.

1. Using a colored pencil, color in the Caribbean cultural realm political entities that had an original dominant Spanish culture. This information can be found in the second column of the table (titled *Original Dominant European Culture*).
2. Using different colored pencils for the other countries in column two, do the same as you did for the Spanish political entities in the above step, but this time shade according to the other original European dominant cultures in the realm.
3. Once you have completed the above two steps, title the map you created "Caribbean Realm Original Dominant European Cultures."
4. Using the other blank map provided, do the same as the above three steps, but this time use the information in the third column (*Current Dominant Culture*) of Table 8-1, and title the map "Caribbean Realm Current Dominant Cultures."

Once you have completed the above steps, study the two maps you have created and answer the following questions.

1. Do you notice a geographic pattern among the original dominant European cultures within the Caribbean Realm? For example, do the political entities appear to be clustered, dispersed, or randomly scattered among the region?

_____

_____

_____

_____

_____

2. What do you think accounts for the patterns or lack of a pattern among the original dominant European cultures in this region?

_____

_____

_____

_____

3. Do you notice a geographic pattern among the current dominant cultures within the Caribbean Realm? Once again, do the political entities appear to be clustered, dispersed, or randomly scattered among the region?

_____

_____

_____

_____

_____

4. What do you think accounts for the patterns or lack of a pattern among the current dominant European cultures in this region?

_____

_____

_____

_____

_____

5. Comparing the maps of the original and current dominant cultures in the Caribbean realm, do you notice any major differences in the dominant cultures among these political entities in the region? If so, where have the major changes occurred?

_____

_____

_____

_____

_____

6. Does there appear to be a geographic pattern associated with these changes? If so, what do you think may account for it? If not, what do you think may account for a lack of a pattern?

_____

_____

_____

_____

_____

_____

_____

Map 3.3

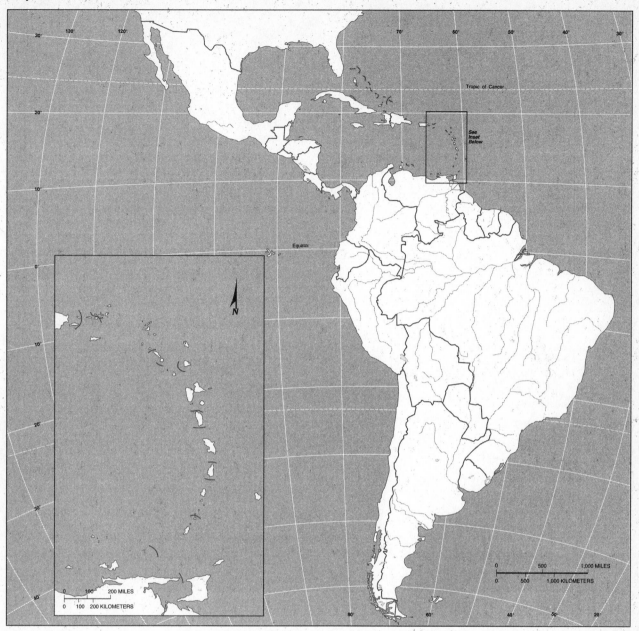

Map 3.4

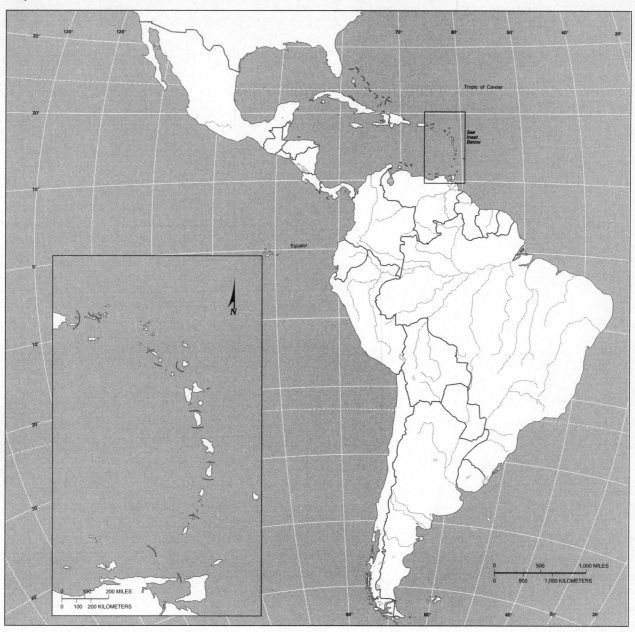

South American Population and Physical Features

Complete the following exercise, using Figure 9-2, Major physiographic regions of South America (page 219); Figure 9-5, Population distribution in South America (page 224); and the blank map provided (workbook Map 3.5).

1. Using Figure 9-2 as a reference, label in the following physical features on the blank map provided:

- Altiplano
- Amazon Basin
- Amazon River
- Andes Mountains
- Atacama Desert
- Brazilian Highlands
- Golfo San Jorge
- Gran Chaco
- Guajira Peninsula
- Guiana Highlands
- La Montana
- Lagos dos Patos
- Llanos
- Llanos De Mojos
- Ilha de Marajo

- Mato Grosso Plateau
- Oriente
- Pampa
- Parana Plateau
- Patagonian Plateau
- Rio Colorado
- Rio de la Plata
- RioNegro
- Rio Orinoco
- Rio Paraguay
- Rio Parana
- Rio Uruguay
- Sertao
- Valle de Chile
- Yungas

Once you have done the above, compare the map you have created with Figure 9-5 and then answer the following questions.

1. Where are the South American regions that possess the highest population densities?

_____

_____

_____

_____

_____

2. Does there appear to be a correlation with high population density regions and South American physical features? If so, what are these features and why do you believe that they have an influence on population clustering?

_____

_____

_____

_____

3. Where are the South American regions that possess the lowest population densities?

_____

_____

_____

_____

_____

4. Does there appear to be a correlation with low population density regions and South American physical features? If so, what are these features and why do you believe that they have an influence on dispersing population?

_____

_____

_____

_____

5. Do either of the above patterns seem to contradict what you would believe to be a logical relationship between population density and physical features? If so, specifically what are the contradictions?

_____

_____

_____

_____

_____

Map 3.5

Map Identification and Exercises for Part 4: Europe

Identify the following features on workbook Maps 4.1 and 4.2

Locate the following countries on Map 4.1

- Albania
- Andorra
- Austria
- Belgium
- Bosnia & Herzegovina
- Bulgaria
- Croatia
- Czechia
- Denmark
- Estonia
- Finland
- France
- Germany
- Greece
- Greenland
- Hungary
- Iceland
- Ireland
- Italy
- Latvia

- Liechtenstein
- Lithuania
- Luxembourg
- Macedonia
- Malta
- Moldova
- Monaco
- Netherlands
- Norway
- Poland
- Portugal
- Romania
- Slovakia
- Slovenia
- Spain
- Sweden
- Switzerland
- United Kingdom
- Yugoslavia

Locate the following cities on Map 4.2

- Amsterdam
- Athens
- Barcelona
- Belfast
- Belgrade
- Berlin
- Bern
- Birmingham
- Bordeaux
- Bratislava
- Bremen
- Brest
- Brussels
- Bucharest
- Budapest
- Copenhagen
- Dublin
- Essen
- Frankfurt
- Geneva
- Genoa
- Glasgow
- Goteborg
- Hamburg
- Hannover
- Helsinki
- Kishinev

- Leeds
- Leipzig
- Lisbon
- Ljubljana
- Lodz
- London
- Luxembourg
- Lyon
- Madrid
- Malaga
- Marseille
- Milan
- Munich
- Naples
- Nice
- Oslo
- Palermo
- Paris
- Porto
- Prague
- Reykjavik
- Riga
- Rome
- Rotterdam
- San Marino
- Sarajevo
- Sevilla

- Krakow
- Skopje
- Sofia
- Stockholm
- Stuttgart
- Tallinn
- Thessaloniki
- Tirana
- Torino
- Toulouse

- Sheffield
- Valencia
- Valletta
- Vienna
- Vilnius
- Warsaw
- Wroclaw
- Zagreb
- Zaragoza
- Zurich

Locate the following physical features on Map 4.2

- Balkan Peninsula
- Northern European Plain
- Iberian Peninsula
- Lapland
- Balearic Islands
- Corsica
- Crete
- Faroe Islands
- Orkney Islands
- Sardinia
- Shetland Islands
- Sicily
- Alps
- Apennines Mountains
- Carpathian Mountains
- Mount Blanc
- Pyrenees Mountains
- Danube River
- Ebro River
- Elbe River

- Garonne River
- Loire River
- Oder River
- Po River
- Rhine River
- Rhone River
- Seine River
- Tagus River
- Thames River
- Vistula River
- Adriatic Sea
- Aegean Sea
- Atlantic Ocean
- Baltic Sea
- Bay of Biscay
- English Channel
- Mediterranean Sea
- North Sea
- Norwegian Sea
- Strait of Gibraltar

Map 4.1

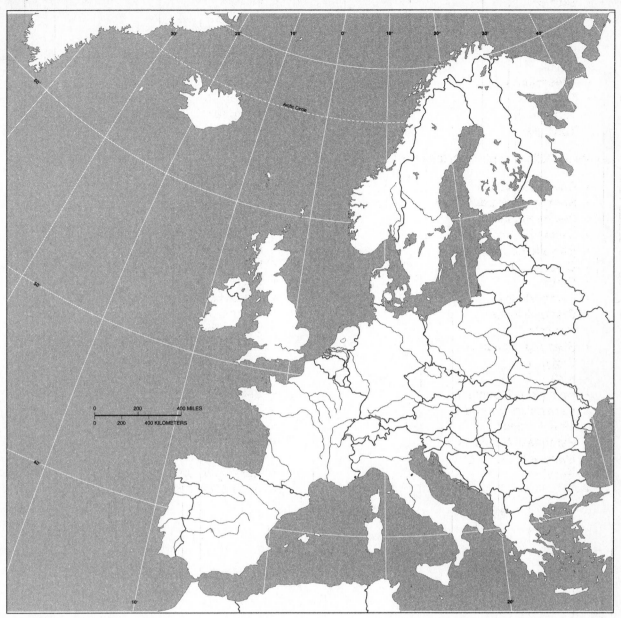

Map 4.2

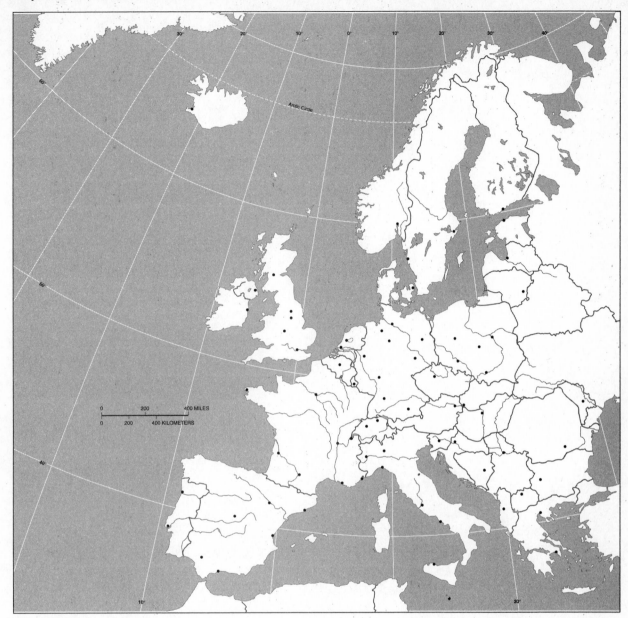

European Environmental Hazards

Using Figure 10-15, Environmental crises and disasters of Europe, on page 261 of your textbook, label the following on the blank map provided (workbook Map 4.3):

1. The approximate European areas affected by forest death.
2. Region of highest concentration of acid rain.
3. Region possessing the worst lead and cadium pollution of the air.
4. The Black Triangle.

Once you have created your map, answer the following questions.

1. Does the region of the greatest concentration of forest death coincide with the region that receives the greatest amount of acid rain? Briefly describe the pattern.

   _____
   _____
   _____
   _____
   _____

2. Are there areas outside of the region of the highest concentration of acid rain that have experienced forest death? If so, what do you think is the cause of forest death in these areas?

   _____
   _____
   _____
   _____
   _____

3. Which countries fall within the Black Triangle?

   _____
   _____
   _____
   _____
   _____

4. Why do you think the Black Triangle is in this region of Europe?

   _____
   _____
   _____
   _____
   _____

5. Where and what are the major industries that have contributed to the environmental crises in the Black Triangle and the overall region of greatest forest death?

_____
_____
_____
_____
_____
_____
_____
_____
_____
_____

Map 4.3

European Language and Religion Patterns

Complete the following exercise, using workbook Map 4.4, Figure 11-2, Major religions of Europe (page 267); and Figure 11-4, Principal languages of Europe (Page 269).

Using Figure 11-2, Major religions of Europe as a reference, label the following on Map 4.4

1. The countries that possess a Protestant majority with a large letter "P."
2. The countries that possess a Catholic majority with a large letter "C."
3. The countries that possess an Eastern Orthodox majority with a large letter "O."
4. The countries that possess an Islamic majority with a large letter "I."
5. The countries that possess a no religious affiliation majority with a large letter "N."

Using Figure 11-4, Principal languages of Europe as a reference, label the following on Map 4.4:

1. Label the countries that predominately speak Romanic languages with a large letter "R."
2. Label the countries that predominately speak Germanic languages with a large letter "G."
3. Label the countries that predominately speak Slavic languages with a large letter "S."

Once you have done the above, study the map you created and answer the following questions.

1. Do you notice any overall patterns of clustering of language families in Europe (i.e., are all the Germanic languages clustered together)? If so, what do you think accounts for these patterns?

_____

_____

_____

_____

_____

2. Do you notice any overall patterns of clustering of religions in Europe (i.e., are all the Protestants clustered together)? If so, what do you think accounts for these patterns?

_____

_____

_____

_____

_____

3. Do you notice any correlations between certain subdivisions of language families and predominant religions practiced in European countries? If so, in which countries do these correlations exist?

_____

_____

_____

_____

_____

4. If you answered yes to the above question, what do you think accounts for the correlations?

_____

_____

_____

_____

_____

5. Which European countries possess non Indo-European language-speaking majorities?

_____

_____

_____

_____

_____

6. Do you see a correlation between language and religion in the non Indo-European language speaking countries? If so, what are they and what do you think accounts for them? If not, why do you think they are different?

_____

_____

_____

_____

_____

Map 4.4

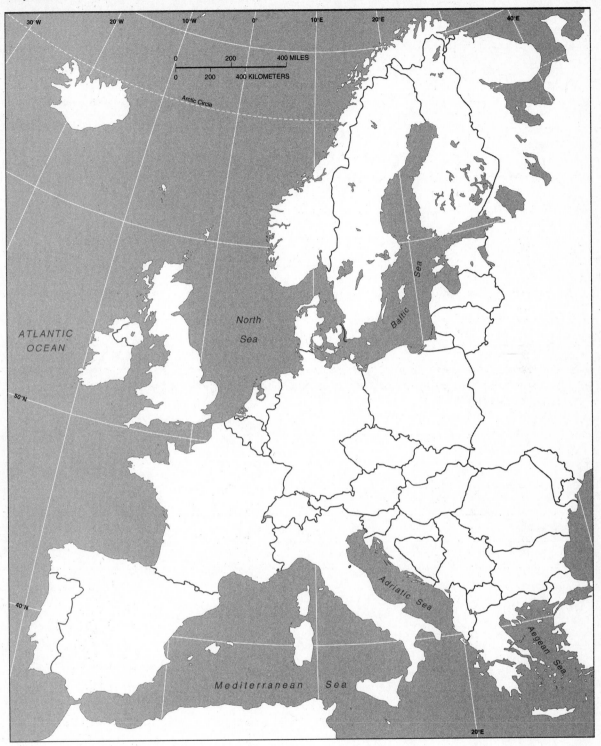

ATLANTIC
OCEAN

North
Sea

Baltic
Sea

Arctic Circle

30°W   20°W   10°W   0°   10°E   20°E   40°E

0   200   400 MILES
0   200   400 KILOMETERS

50°N

40°N

Adriatic Sea

Aegean Sea

Mediterranean   Sea

20°E

Map Identification and Exercises for Part 5: Russia and Central Eurasia

Identify the following features on workbook Maps 5.1 and 5.2

Identify and label the following countries on Map 5.1

- Afghanistan
- Armenia
- Azerbaijan
- Belarus
- Georgia
- Kazakhstan
- Kyrgyzstan
- Russia
- Tajikistan
- Turkmenistan
- Ukraine
- Uzbekistan

Identify and label the following cities on Map 5.2

- Almaty
- Ashgabat
- Astana
- Baki (Baku)
- Bishkek
- Donetsk
- Dushanbe
- Groznyy
- Irkutsk
- Kazan
- Khabarovsk
- Kharkov
- Kiev
- Minsk
- Moscow
- Kabul
- Niznij Novgorod
- Norilsk
- Novosibirsk
- Odessa
- Omsk
- Samara
- St. Petersburg
- Tashkent
- Tbilisi
- Verkhoyansk
- Vladivostok
- Volgograd
- Yakutsk
- Yerevan

Identify and label the following physical features on Map 5.2

- Amu Darya River
- Amur River
- Aral Sea
- Arctic Ocean
- Baltic Sea
- Barents Sea
- Bering Sea
- Black Sea
- Caspian Sea
- Dnieper River
- Lake Baikal
- Lake Balkhash
- Lena River
- North Sea
- Ob River
- Pacific Ocean
- Sea of Japan
- Sea of Okhotsk
- Syr Darya River
- Volga River
- Yenisey River
- Caucasus Mountains
- Kamchatka Peninsula
- Kola Peninsula
- Kuril Islands
- Novaya Zemlya
- Pamir Mountains
- Sakhalin Island
- Siberia
- Ural Mountains
- Verkhoyansk Range
- Yakutsk Basin

Map 5.1

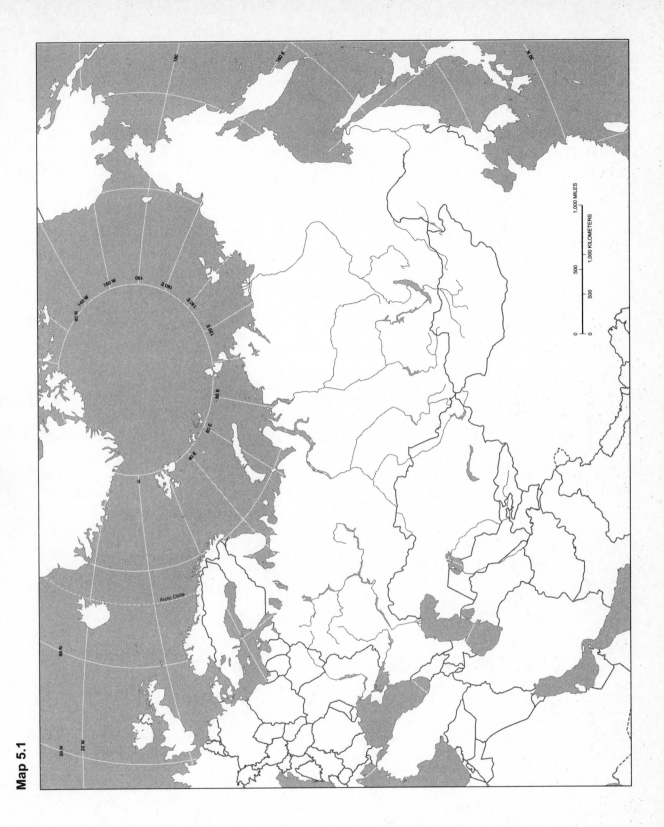

Map 5.2

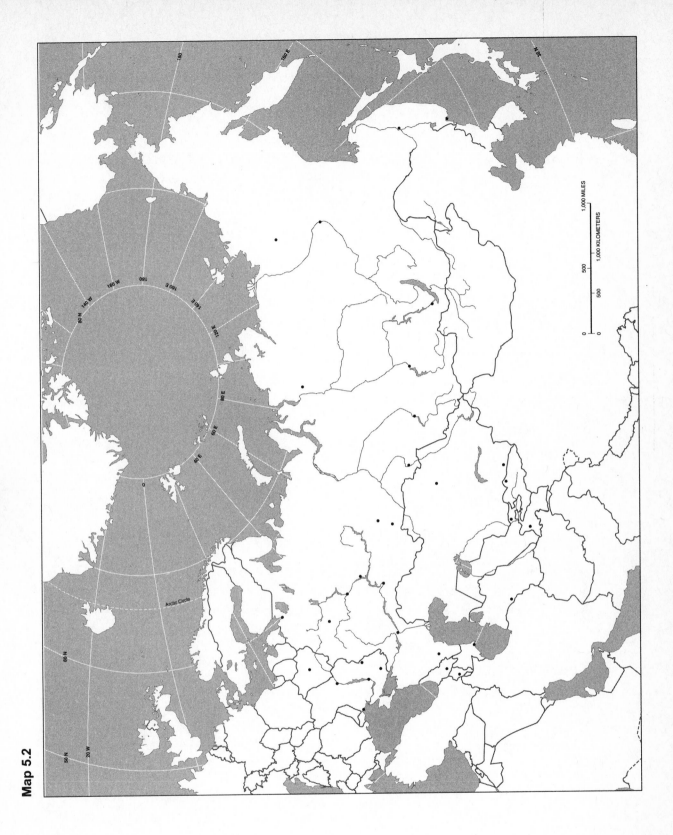

Arctic Circle

1,000 MILES
1,000 KILOMETERS
500
500

Non-Russian Ethnic Groups in Russia

Using Figure 14-4, Percentage of non-Russian ethnic groups in Russia (page 328), and the blank map provided (workbook Map 5.3), complete the below following exercise.

1. On the blank map, use a colored pencil to shade in the approximate Russian regions that are 50% or greater non-Russian.
2. Using a different colored pencil, shade in the approximate Russian regions that are 25-49% non-Russian.
3. Using a different colored pencil, shade in the approximate Russian regions that are 10-24% non-Russian.

After you have created your map, study it and answer the following questions.

1. Where are the regions of the highest non-Russian concentration in Russia?

_____

_____

_____

_____

_____

_____

2. Where are these regions in relation to the borders of the former U.S.S.R?

_____

_____

_____

_____

_____

3. Is there an overall clustering of Russia's non-European majority? If so, what is it?

_____

_____

_____

_____

_____

4. In what ways has the pattern of non-Russian ethnicities in Russia generated conflict in the country?

_____

_____

_____

_____

_____

_____

_____

5. Would the pattern of non-Russian ethnicities in Russia readily permit the separation of these individuals into their own states?

_____

_____

_____

_____

_____

_____

_____

_____

Map 5.3

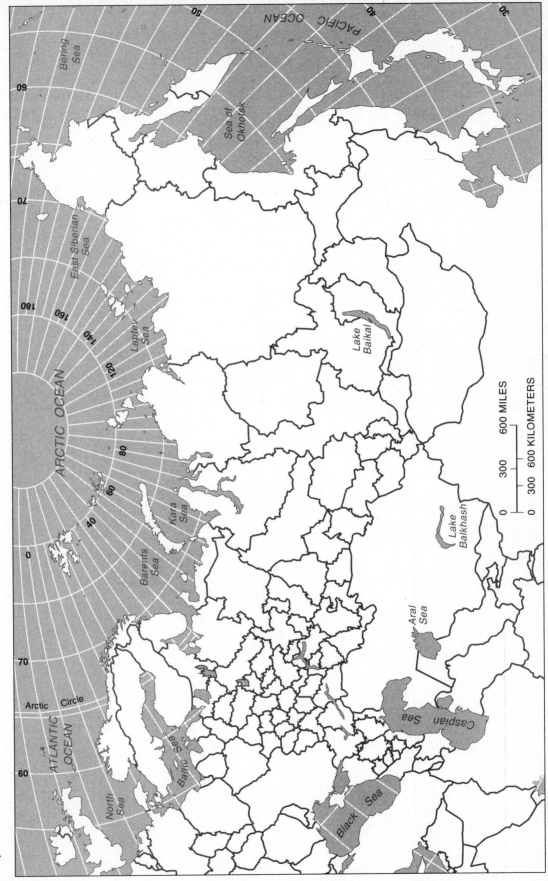

Desiccation of the Aral Sea

From your textbook read the Geography In Action box *The Aral Sea* on pages 348 and 349. Once you have done this, complete the below exercise.

Using Figure C, Projected area of the Aral Sea in 2010, if loss of water intake is not controlled (page 349), and the blank map provided (workbook Map 5.4), do the following:

1. Shade in and label the area representing the 1960 land fill area.
2. Shade in and label the area representing the land fill area in 1978.
3. Shade in and label the area representing the land fill area today.
4. Shade in and label the area representing the predicted 2010 land fill area.
5. Draw lines representing the approximate locations of the Amu Darya and Syr Darya Rivers.

Once you have done the above, study the map you created and answer the following questions.

1. Using the provided scale on the map, starting from the sea's eastern shore measure the amount of retreat of the Aral Sea from 1960 to 1978. Approximately how many miles has the sea retreated during this period?

_____

_____

_____

2. Using the provided scale on the map, from the east measure the amount of retreat of the Aral Sea from 1978 to today. Approximately how many miles has the sea retreated during this period?

_____

_____

_____

3. Using the provided scale on the map, from the east measure the amount of retreat of the Aral Sea from today to the projected 2010 shoreline location. Approximately how many miles has the sea retreated during this period?

_____

_____

_____

4. Which of the above three periods has seen, or will have seen the greatest amount of surface area loss?

_____

_____

_____

5. What is the primary cause of loss of water to the Aral Sea?

_____

_____

_____

_____

6. How has this shoreline retreat had an effect on the surrounding region?

_____

_____

_____

_____

_____

_____

_____

Map 5.4

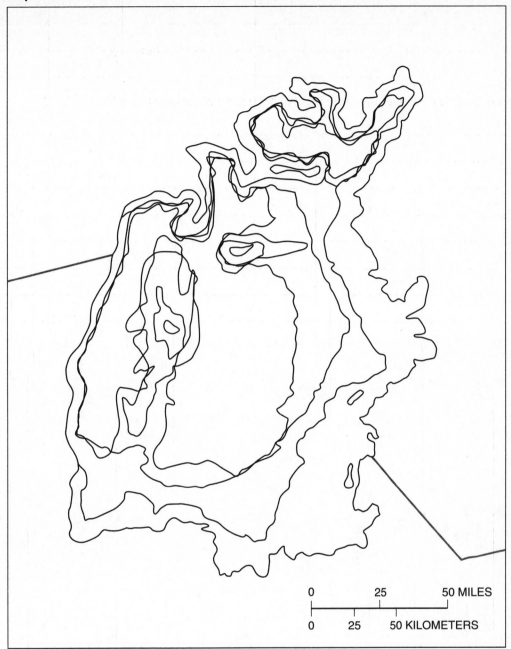

0   25   50 MILES

0   25   50 KILOMETERS

Map Identification and Exercises for Part 6: Australia, New Zealand, and the Pacific Islands

Identify the following features on workbook Maps 6.1 and 6.2

Identify and label the following countries on Map 6.1

- American Samoa
- Australia
- Caroline Islands
- Cook Islands
- Federated States of Micronesia
- Fiji
- French Polynesia
- Guam
- Kiribati
- Marquesas Islands
- Marshall Islands
- Nauru
- New Caledonia
- New Zealand
- Niue
- Palau
- Papua New Guinea
- Samoa
- Society Islands
- Solomon Islands
- Tokelau
- Tonga
- Tuvalu
- Vanuatu
- Wallis and Futuna

Identify and label the following cities on Map 6.2

- Adelaide
- Apia
- Auckland
- Brisbane
- Canberra
- Cairns
- Christchurch
- Funafuti
- Hobart
- Honiara
- Koror
- Majuro
- Melbourne
- Moorea
- Noumea
- Nuku'alofa
- Palikir
- Perth
- Port Moresby
- Port-Vila
- Suva
- Sydney
- Tarawa
- Wellington
- Yaren

Identify and label the following physical features on Map 6.2

- Darling Ranges
- Flinders Range
- Great Artesian Basin
- Great Dividing Range
- Great Sandy Desert
- Great Victoria Desert
- MacDonnell Range
- Arafura Sea
- Coral Sea
- Darling River
- Indian Ocean
- Murray River
- Southern Ocean
- Tasman Sea
- Melanesia
- Micronesia
- Polynesia
- Tasmania

Map 6.1

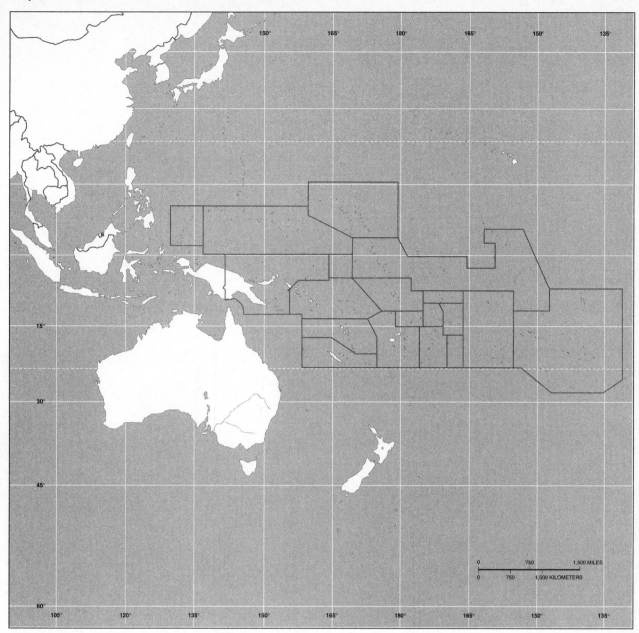

Map 6.2

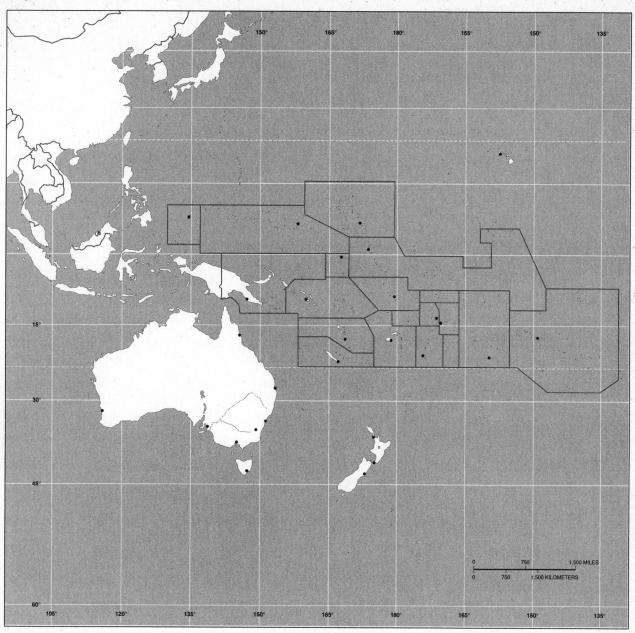

Australian Settlement Patterns

Complete the following exercise, using Figure 16-1, Selected cities and population distribution of Australia and New Zealand (page 360); Figure 16-2, Natural regions and precipitation in Australia and New Zealand (page 361); Figure 16-9 Rural land use and mineral resources of Australia and New Zealand (page 366); and the blank map provided (workbook Map 6.3).

1. Using Figure 16-1 as a reference, label in the Australian features listed below on the blank map provided:

   - Arafura Sea
   - Bass Strait
   - Cape York Peninsula
   - Coral Sea
   - Darling River
   - Great Australian Bight
   - Great Barrier Reef
   - Gulf of Carpentaria
   - Indian Ocean
   - Kimberly Plateau
   - Lake Eyre Basin

   - New South Wales
   - Northern Territory
   - Ord River
   - Pilbara Coast
   - Queensland
   - South Australia
   - Spencer Gulf
   - Tasmania
   - Timor Sea
   - Victoria
   - Western Australia

2. Shade in areas of major Australia urban concentration.
3. Using Figure 16-2 as a reference, draw and label lines to indicate regions that receive 60 or more inches of annual precipitation.
4. Do the same as above for the regions that receive 40, 20, and 10 inches of annual precipitation.

Once you have done the above, study the map you have created and answer the following questions.

1. Where are the Australian regions of highest urban concentration?

_____

_____

_____

_____

2. Does there appear to be a geographic pattern among Australian cities? If so, what is it?

_____

_____

_____

3. What do you think accounts for the patterns of Australian urban concentration? Do physical factors appear to play a role?

_____

_____

_____

_____

_____

4. Thinking about the above question, could you formulize a generalization regarding Australian settlement and climate?

_____

_____

_____

_____

_____

Now briefly study Figure 16-9, Rural land use and mineral resources of Australia and New Zealand, compare it with the map you created, and answer questions 5, 6, and 7.

5. How does Australian rural land use correlate with climate?

_____

_____

_____

_____

_____

6. Do you see a pattern regarding climate and rural land use in Australia? If so, what is that pattern?

_____

_____

_____

_____

_____

7. If you compare Figure 16-9 with your map you will notice that the Australian regions that possess the harshest climatic conditions still contain pockets of economic activity. What are these activities?

_____

_____

_____

_____

_____

8. Why are these economic activities possible in these regions?

_____

_____

_____

_____

_____

Map 6.3

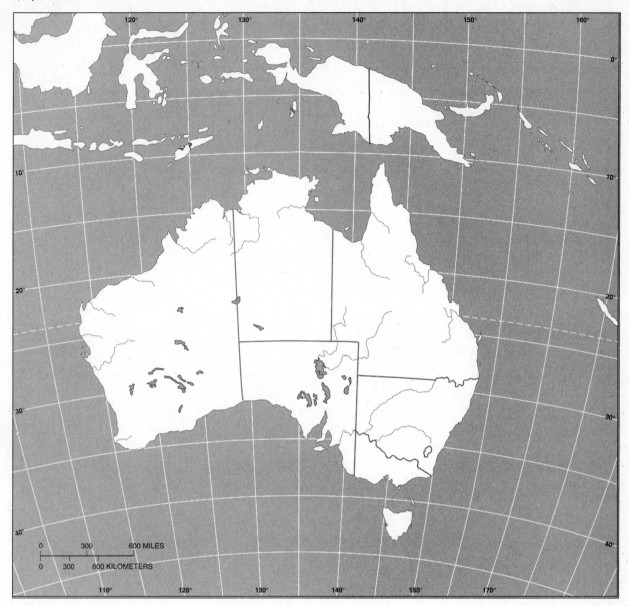

Pacific Island Realm Political Geography

Complete the following exercise, using Figure 16-13, Pacific Island Realm (page 372); Table 16-1, The Pacific Islands (page 373); and the blank map provided (workbook Map 6.4).

1. On the blank map, draw a line encompassing the Pacific islands that are part of Melanesia.
2. Draw a line encompassing the Pacific islands that are part of Micronesia.
3. Draw a line encompassing the Pacific islands that are part of Polynesia.
4. Label the above three regions.

Using Table 16-1 as a reference, complete steps 5 and 6.

5. Using a colored pencil, shade in the islands that possess an independent political structure (found in column two of the table).
6. Using different colored pencils, shade in the other Pacific islands according to their respective political structures.

Once you have completed the above steps, study your map and answer the following questions.

1. What are the general locations of the islands of Melanesia, Micronesia, and Polynesia?

_____

_____

_____

_____

_____

2. What are the characteristics of these islands that give them the names Melanesia, Micronesia, and Polynesia?

_____

_____

_____

_____

_____

3. Do you notice a geographic pattern among the political structure of the Pacific islands? If so, what is it?

_____

_____

_____

_____

_____

4. What do you think accounts for the pattern of the political structure of the Pacific islands? If there is no pattern displayed, what do you think accounts for a lack of a pattern?

_____

_____

_____

_____

_____

_____

_____

_____

_____

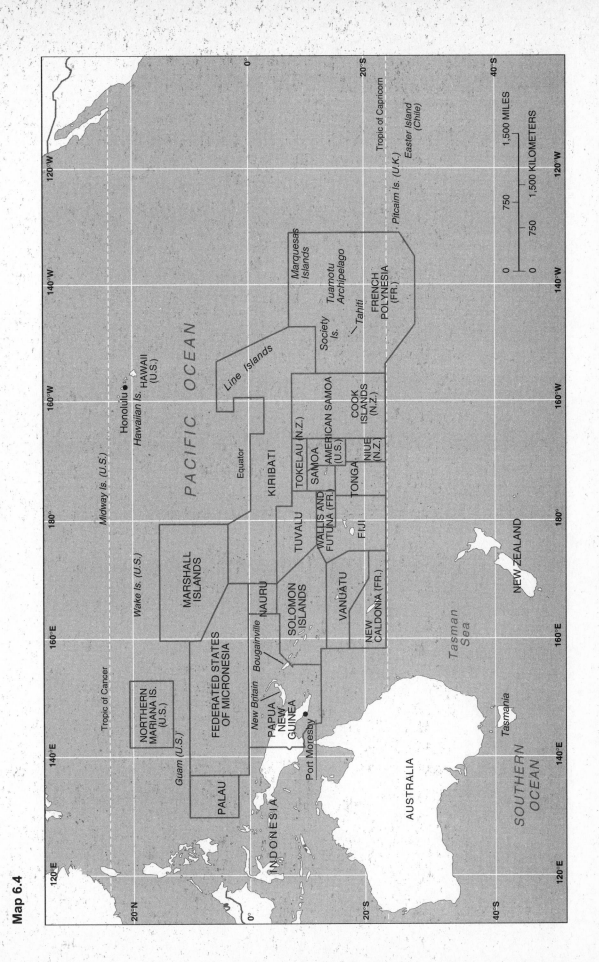

Map 6.4

Map Identification and Exercises for Part 7: Asia

Identify the following features on workbook Maps 7.1 and 7.2

Identify and label the following countries on Map 7.1

- Malaysia
- Bangladesh
- Bhutan
- Brunei
- Burma (Myanmar)
- Cambodia
- China
- East Timor
- India
- Indonesia
- Japan
- Laos
- Maldives
- Nepal
- North Korea
- Pakistan
- Philippines
- Singapore
- South Korea
- Sri Lanka
- Taiwan
- Thailand
- Vietnam

Identify and label the following cities on Map 7.2

- Bangalore
- Bangkok
- Beijing
- Colombo
- Dhaka
- Dili
- Guangzhou
- Ha Noi
- Ho Chi Min City
- Hong Kong
- Hyderabad
- Islamabad
- Jakarta
- Taipei
- Karachi
- Katmandu
- Kobe
- Kolkata (Calcutta)
- Kyoto
- Lahore
- Lhasa
- Madras
- Male
- Manila
- Mumbai
- Nanjing
- New Deli
- Osaka
- P'yongyang
- Phnom Penh
- Seoul
- Shanghai
- Thimphu
- Tokyo
- Vientiane
- Yangon

Identify and label the following physical features on Map 7.2

- Altay Mountains
- Deccan Plateau
- Eastern Ghats
- Gobi Desert
- Himalayas
- Hindu Kush
- Kunlun Mountains
- Taklamakan Desert
- Tian Shan
- Tibetan Plateau
- Western Ghats
- Adaman Sea
- Arabian Sea
- South China Sea
- Bay of Bengal
- Brahmaputra River
- Celebes Sea
- Chang Jiang River
- East China Sea
- Ganges River
- Huang He River
- Indian Ocean
- Indus River
- Java Sea
- Mekong River
- Philippine Sea
- Sea of Japan
- Java

- Yellow Sea
- Borneo
- Hainan
- Hokkaido
- Honshu

- Kyushu
- Luzon
- Mindanao
- Shikoku
- Sumatra

Map 7.1

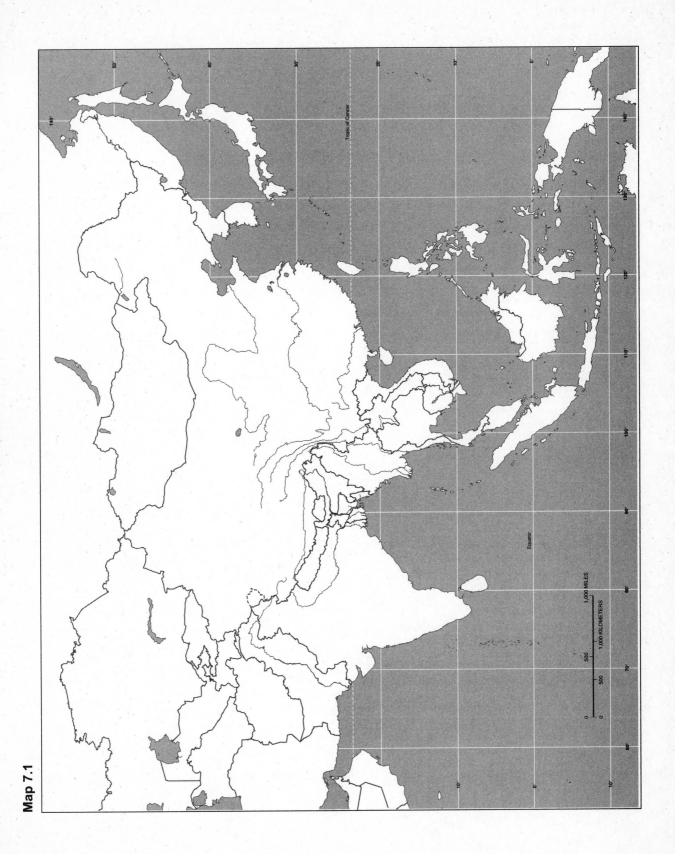

Map 7.2

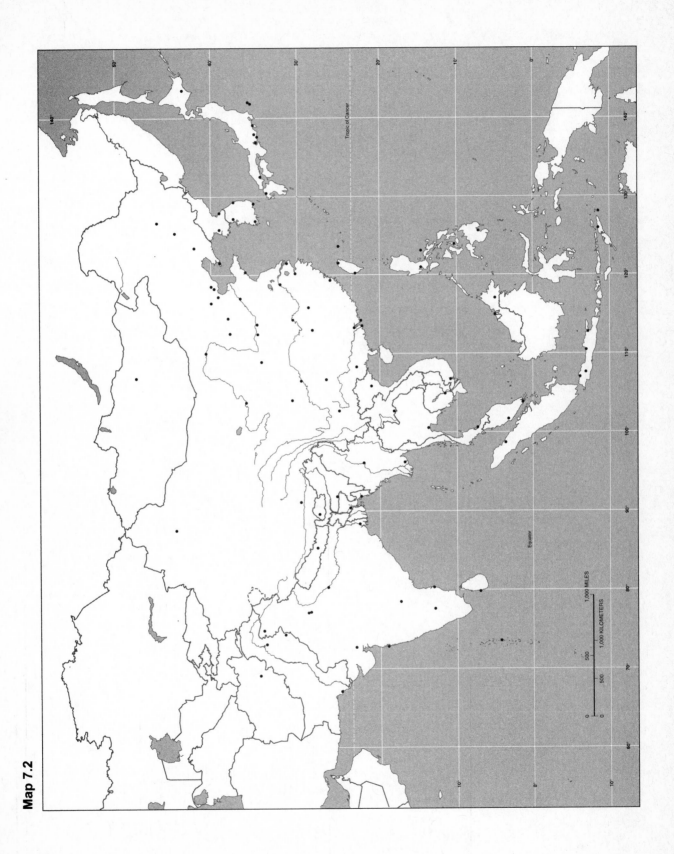

The Asian Monsoon

Complete the following exercise, using Figure 17-2, Annual rainfall and dominant atmospheric streamlines over monsoon Asia during the summer (page 383); Figure 17-3, Annual rainfall and dominant atmospheric streamlines over monsoon Asia during the winter (page 384); and workbook Maps 7.3 and 7.4.

Title Map 7.3 "Asian Winter Monsoon" and indicate the following on it:

1. Area of predominant high pressure.
2. Predominant wind direction.
3. Regions receiving high precipitation (if relevant).

Title Map 7.4 "Asian Summer Monsoon" and indicate the following on it:

4. Area of predominant low pressure.
5. Predominant wind direction.
6. Regions receiving high precipitation (if relevant).

Once you have done the above, study the maps you have created and answer the following questions.

1. During the Asian winter, from what direction do the prevailing winds originate?

_____

_____

_____

_____

_____

_____

_____

2. During the Asian summer, from what direction do the prevailing winds originate?

_____

_____

_____

_____

_____

_____

_____

3. What would be the moisture characteristics of the winter and summer winds?

_____

_____

_____

_____

_____

_____

_____

4. Giving the seasonal shifting patterns of winds, what are the general regional patterns of precipitation in Asia?

_____

_____

_____

_____

_____

_____

_____

5. Given your knowledge of the Asian monsoon, do you think there are regions within Asia that receive more consistent amounts of precipitation throughout the year? If yes, where do you think they are?

_____

_____

_____

_____

_____

_____

_____

Map 7.3

Season: _____

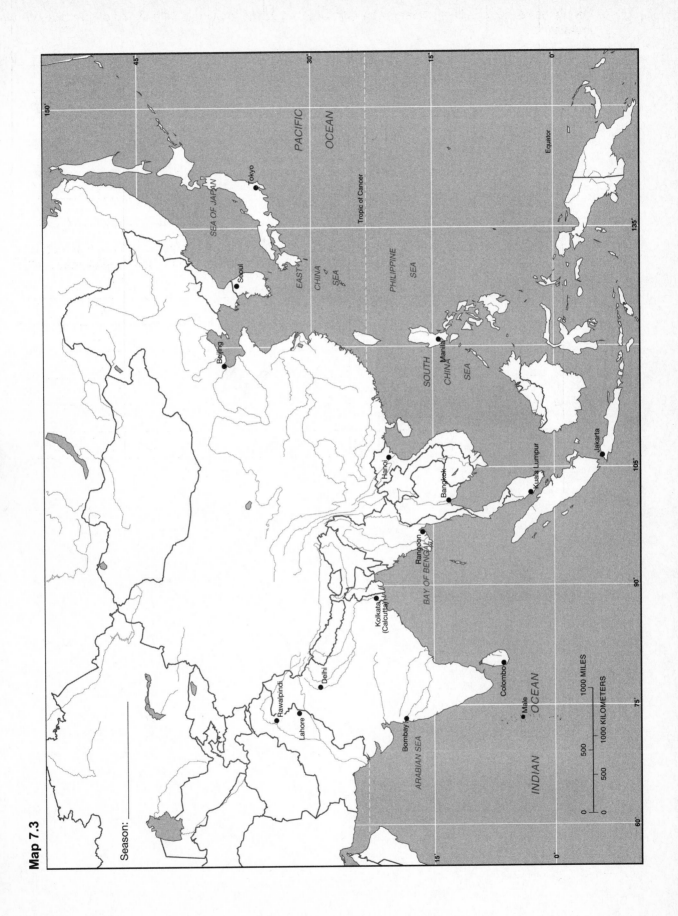

Map 7.4

Season: _____

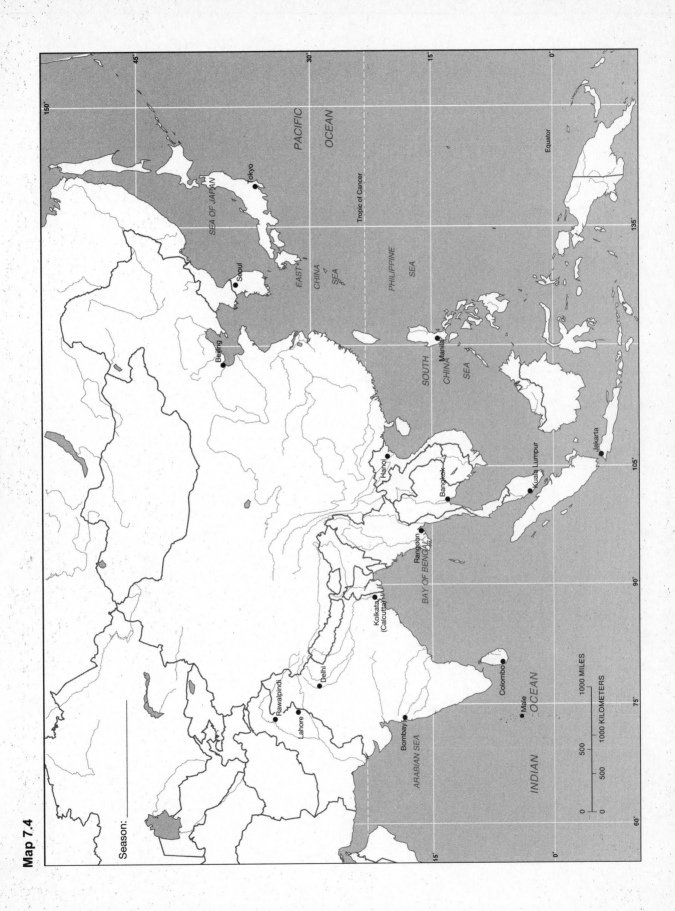

Populated and Unpopulated Regions of Asia

Using Figure 17-6, Population distribution of Asia, East by South (page 388), and the blank map provided (workbook Map 7.5), complete the following exercise.

1. On the blank map, shade in the regions that appear to possess high population densities.
2. Using a different colored pencil, shade in the regions that are populated but appear to possess lower densities than the identified regions in question #1.

Once you have done the above, study the map you have created, compare it with the physical map of Asia (found at the beginning of the chapter on pages 378-379), and answer the following questions.

1. Where are the Asian regions that possess the highest population densities?

_____

_____

_____

_____

_____

2. What do you think accounts for the clustering of people into these regions?

_____

_____

_____

_____

_____

3. Do physical features seem to play a role in high population densities? If so, what are the physical characteristics of the landscape that appear to promote population?

_____

_____

_____

_____

_____

4. Where are the Asian regions that possess the lowest population densities?

_____

_____

_____

_____

_____

5. What do you think accounts for the clustering of people into these regions?

_____

_____

_____

_____

_____

_____

6. Do physical features seem to play a role in low population densities? If so, what are the physical characteristics of the landscape that appear to limit population?

_____

_____

_____

_____

_____

_____

Map 7.5

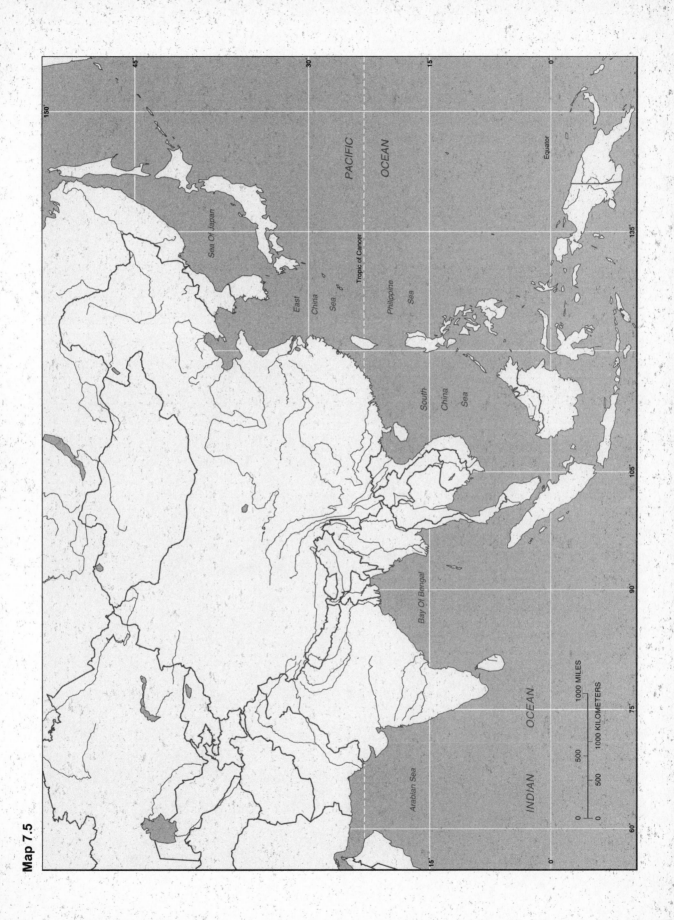

Sea Of Japan

PACIFIC

OCEAN

Tropic of Cancer

East
China
Sea

Philippine
Sea

South
China
Sea

Bay Of Bengal

Equator

Arabian Sea

INDIAN   OCEAN

1000 MILES
1000 KILOMETERS
500
500
0
0

Map Identification and Exercises for Part 8: The Middle East and North Africa

Identify the following features on workbook Maps 8.1 and 8.2

Identify and label the following countries on Map 8.1

- Algeria
- Bahrain
- Egypt
- Gaza
- Iran
- Iraq
- Israel
- Jordan
- Kuwait
- Lebanon
- Libya
- Morocco
- Oman
- Qatar
- Saudi Arabia
- Syria
- Tunisia
- Turkey
- United Arab Emirates
- West Bank
- Yemen

Identify and label the following cities on Map 8.2

- Abu Dhabi
- Algiers
- Amman
- Ankara
- Aswan
- Baghdad
- Basra
- Beirut
- Cairo
- Damascus
- Doha
- El Aaiun
- Fez
- Istanbul
- Jerusalem
- Kuwait
- Manama
- Marrakech
- Mecca
- Medina
- Mosul
- Muscat
- Nicosia
- Rabat
- Riyadh
- San'a
- Tabriz
- Tehran
- Tel Aviv
- Tripoli
- Tunis

Identify and label the following physical features on Map 8.2

- Ahaggar Highlands
- Atlas Mountains
- Elburz Mountains
- Zagros Mountains
- Anatolian Plateau
- Arabian Peninsula
- Iranian Plateau
- Qattara Depression
- Rub-Al-Khali
- Sinai Peninsula
- Socotra
- Atlantic Ocean
- Black Sea
- Caspian Sea
- Euphrates River
- Indian Ocean
- Mediterranean Sea
- Nile River
- Persian Gulf
- Red Sea
- Tigris River

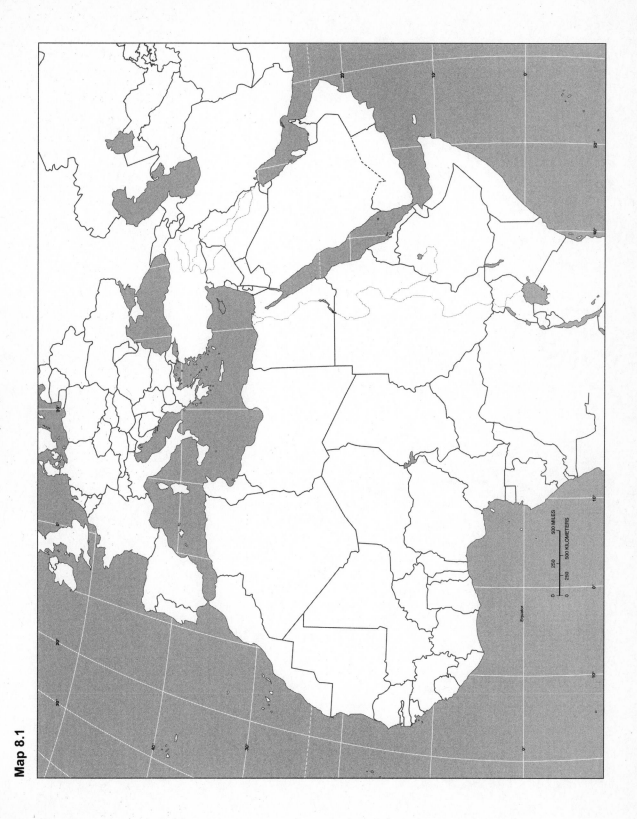

Map 8.1

Map 8.2

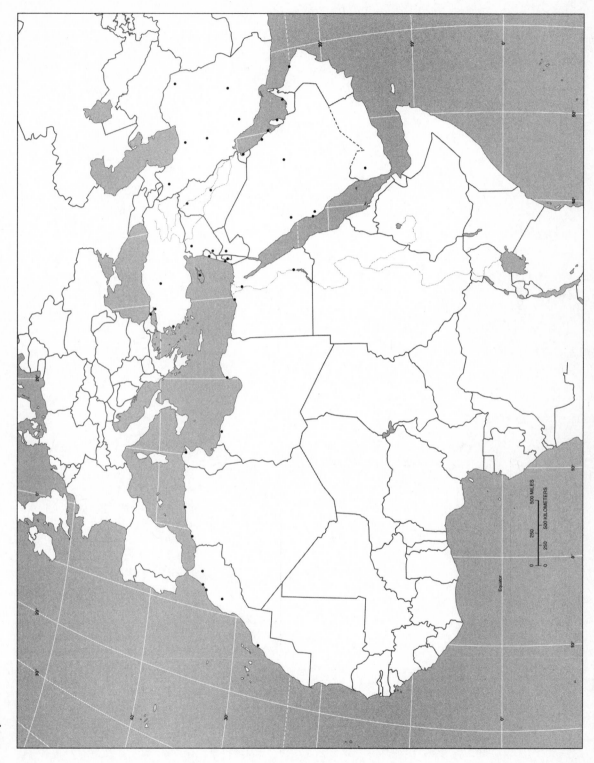

Population and Petroleum Production in the Middle East and North Africa

Complete the following exercise, using Table 23-2, Population and Petroleum Production in the Mediterranean Crescent Countries (page 545); Table 24-1, Population and Petroleum Production in the Gulf States (page 562); and the blank map provided (workbook Map 8.3).

1. Using a colored pencil, shade in the countries that have a year 2000 petroleum production of 15018000 thousands of barrels per day.
2. Using a different colored pencil, shade in the countries that have a year 2000 petroleum production of 501-1500 thousands of barrels per day.
3. Using a different colored pencil, shade in the countries that have a year 2000 petroleum production of 51-500 thousands of barrels per day.
4. Using a different colored pencil, shade in the countries that have a year 2000 petroleum production of 0.1-50 thousands of barrels per day.
5. Label the countries that have a population between 53.2 and 71.2 million with the number 1.
6. Label the countries that have a population between 35.2 and 71.1 million with the number 2.
7. Label the countries that have a population between 17.2 and 35.1 million with the number 3.
8. Label the countries that have a population between 0.7 and 17.1 million with the number 4.

Petroleum Production (in thousand barrels per day)	Color	Population (millions)	Number
1501 to 8000		53.2 to 71.2	1
501 to 1500		35.2 to 53.1	2
51 to 500		17.2 to 35.1	3
0.1 to 50		0.7 to 17.1	4

Once you have done the above, study the map you created and answer the following questions:

1. What are the top four petroleum-producing countries in the region?

_____

_____

_____

_____

_____

_____

2. Do you notice an overall geographic pattern among these high petroleum production countries? If so, where are they?

_____

_____

_____

_____

_____

3. What are the bottom four petroleum-producing countries?

_____

_____

_____

_____

_____

_____

4. Do you notice an overall geographic pattern among low petroleum production countries? If so, where are they?

_____

_____

_____

_____

_____

_____

5. Which countries in the region possess the largest amount of petroleum produced per person (i.e., a correlation between high production and countries labeled with a number 3 or 4)? Do these countries display a geographic pattern?

_____

_____

_____

_____

_____

6. Do you believe that the wealth is distributed evenly in these countries? Why, or why not?

_____

_____

_____

_____

_____

Map 8.3

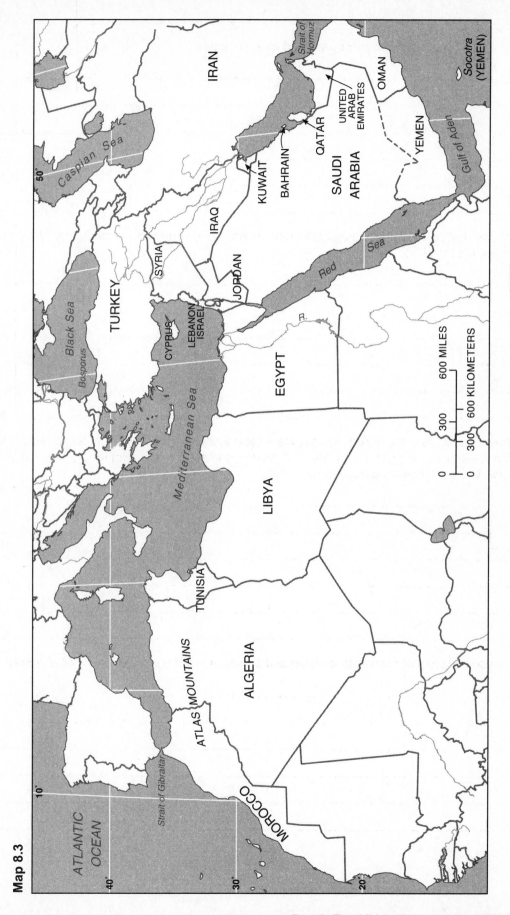

Geographic Patterns of Palestinian Refugees

Using Table 23-5, Estimated Palestinian Refugee Populations (page 557) and the blank map provided (workbook Map 8.4) complete the following exercise.

1. Using a colored pencil, shade in the countries that have a Palestinian refugee population of 1 million or greater.
2. Using a different colored pencil, shade in the countries that have a Palestinian population of 300,000 to 500,000.
3. Using a different colored pencil, shade in the countries that have a Palestinian population of 90,000 to 299,999.
4. Using a different colored pencil, shade in the countries that have a Palestinian population of 150 to 89,999.

Once you have created your map, study it and then answer the following questions.

1. Which countries have the largest number of Palestinian refugees in the region?

_____

_____

_____

_____

2. Which countries have the smallest number of Palestinian refugees in the region?

_____

_____

_____

_____

3. Do you notice a geographic pattern among countries that have a high number of Palestinian refugees? If so, what do you think accounts for these patterns?

_____

_____

_____

_____

_____

4. Do you notice a geographic pattern among countries that have a low number of Palestinian refugees? If so, what do you think accounts for these patterns?

_____

_____

_____

_____

_____

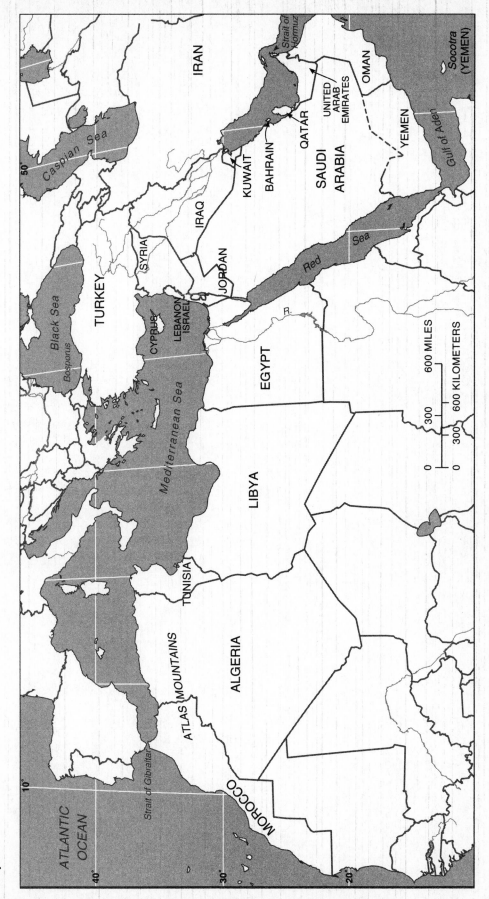

Map 8.4

Map Identification and Exercises for Part 9: Africa South of the Sahara

Identify the following features on workbook Maps 9.1 and 9.2

Identify and label the following countries on Map 9.1

- Angola
- Benin
- Botswana
- Burkina Faso
- Burundi
- Cabinda (Angola)
- Cameroon
- Cape Verde
- Central African Republic
- Chad
- Comoro Islands
- Democratic Republic of Congo
- Djibouti
- Equatorial Guinea
- Eritrea
- Ethiopia
- Gabon
- Gambia
- Ghana
- Guinea
- Guinea-Bissau
- Ivory Coast
- Kenya
- Lesotho
- Liberia
- Madagascar
- Malawi
- Mali
- Mauritania
- Mauritius
- Mozambique
- Namibia
- Niger
- Nigeria
- Republic of the Congo
- Rwanda
- Sao Tome and Principe
- Senegal
- Seychelles
- Sierra Leone
- Somalia
- South Africa
- Sudan
- Swaziland
- Tanzania
- Togo
- Uganda
- Zambia
- Zimbabwe

Identify and label the following cities on Map 9.2

- Abuja
- Accra
- Addis Ababa
- Antananarivo
- Asmara
- Bangui
- Banjul
- Bissau
- Bloemfontein
- Brazzaville
- Bujumbura
- Cape Town
- Conakry
- Dakar
- Dar es Salaam
- Djibouti
- Freetown
- Gaborone
- Harare
- Johannesburg
- Kigali
- Kinshasa
- Lagos
- Libreville
- Lilongwe
- Lome
- Luanda
- Lusaka
- Malabo
- Maputo
- Maseru
- Mbabane
- Mogadishu
- Monrovia
- Moroni
- N'Djamena
- Nairobi
- Niamey
- Nouakchott
- Kampala

- Khartoum
- Praia
- Pretoria
- Tombouctou
- Victoria

- Port Louis
- Porto-Novo
- Windhoek
- Yamoussoukro
- Yaounde

Identify and label the following physical features on Map 9.2

- Atlantic Ocean
- Blue Nile River
- Congo River
- Gulf of Aden
- Gulf of Guinea
- Indian Ocean
- Lake Chad
- Lake Nyasa
- Lake Tanganyika
- Lake Victoria
- Mozambique Channel
- Niger River
- Nile River
- Red Sea

- Senegal River
- White Nile River
- Zambezi River
- Congo Basin
- Drakensberg Mountains
- Ethiopian Highlands
- Great Rift Valley
- Guinea Highlands
- Kalahari Desert
- Katanga Plateau
- Namib Desert
- Nubian Desert
- Sahara Desert
- Somali Peninsula

Map 9.1

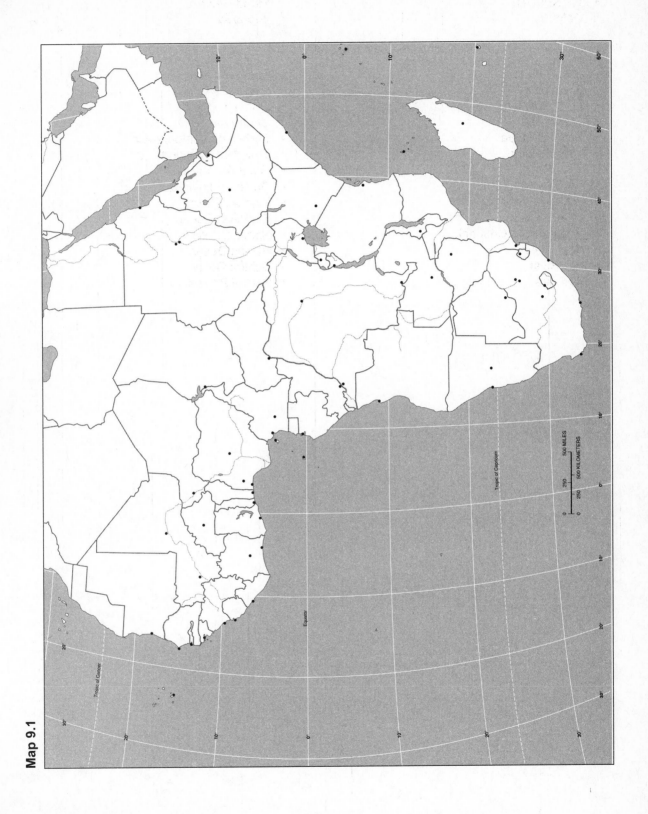

Map 9.2

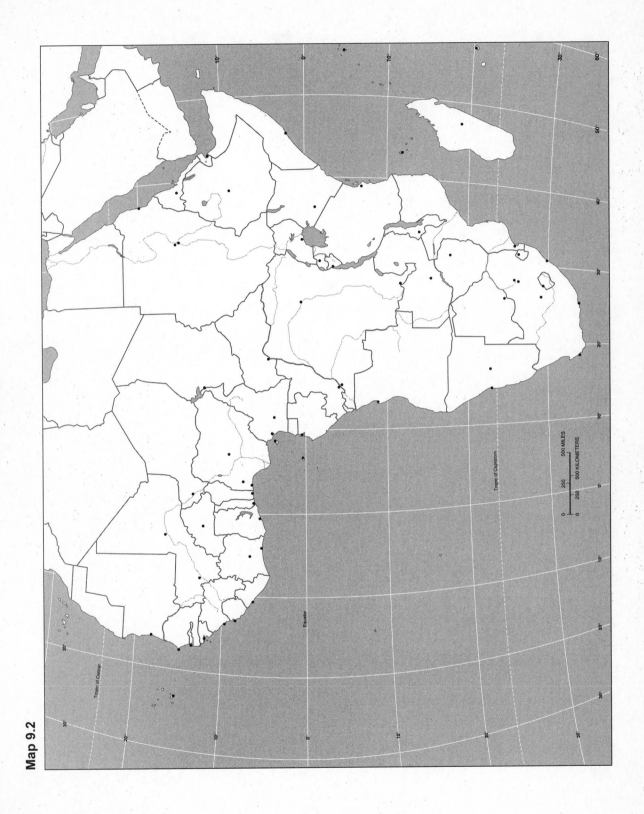

Colonial and Linguistic Borders in Africa, South of the Sahara

Complete the following exercise, using Figure 25-11, Colonial Map of Sub-Saharan Africa, 1956 (page 598); Figure 25-12, Distribution of Languages in Africa (page 600); and the blank map provided (workbook Map 9.3).

1. On the blank map, shade in the approximate borders of the major Sub-Saharan African language groups.

Once you have done the above, answer the following questions.

1. Within each major African linguistic boundary, approximately how many individual languages are there?

_____

_____

_____

_____

_____

2. How dispersed do these languages appear to be within each of these linguistic boundaries?

_____

_____

_____

_____

3. How well do the overall linguistic boundaries you have drawn on the map conform with the national borders established by the African colonial powers? Please describe.

_____

_____

_____

_____

4. How might the linguistic boundaries and the colonial borders prove problematic?

_____

_____

_____

_____

_____

5. Once the colonial powers relinquished their African colonial holdings, why did the African cultures not reestablish the national boundaries based on some cultural attribute such as language?

_____

_____

_____

_____

_____

Map 9.3

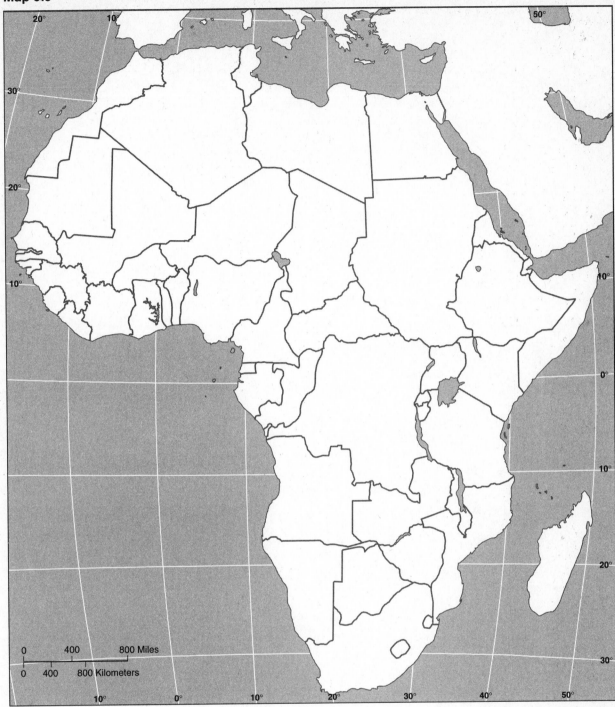

Major African Landforms

Using Figure 26-1, Major landforms in Africa (page 624), as a reference, and the blank map provided (workbook Map 9.4), complete the following exercise.

1. Draw in and label the major African basins, highlands, and plateaus.
2. Draw in and label the major African mountain ranges.
3. Draw in and label the major African river systems.
4. Draw in and label the major African deserts.
5. Draw in and label the major African escarpments.

Once you have done the above, study the map you have created and answer the following questions.

1. Where are the major African basin regions? Do you notice a geographic pattern with these basins?

_____

_____

_____

_____

_____

2. Do the African rivers appear to be influenced by the basins? If so, how?

_____

_____

_____

_____

_____

3. Where are the major African plateaus and highlands located?

_____

_____

_____

_____

_____

4. Where are the major escarpments? Does there appear to be a geographic pattern with these features?

_____

_____

_____

_____

_____

5. What is responsible for the line of escarpments on the east side of the African continent?

_____

_____

_____

_____

_____

6. At approximately what latitudes are the African deserts located? Why do you think they are located at these latitudes?

_____

_____

_____

_____

_____

7. Where are the major African mountain ranges located?

_____

_____

_____

_____

_____

8. In comparison to the other continents, Africa possesses few mountain ranges. Why do you think this is so?

_____

_____

_____

_____

_____

9. Overall, how would you describe the physical landforms of the African continent?

_____

_____

_____

_____

_____

_____

Map 9.4

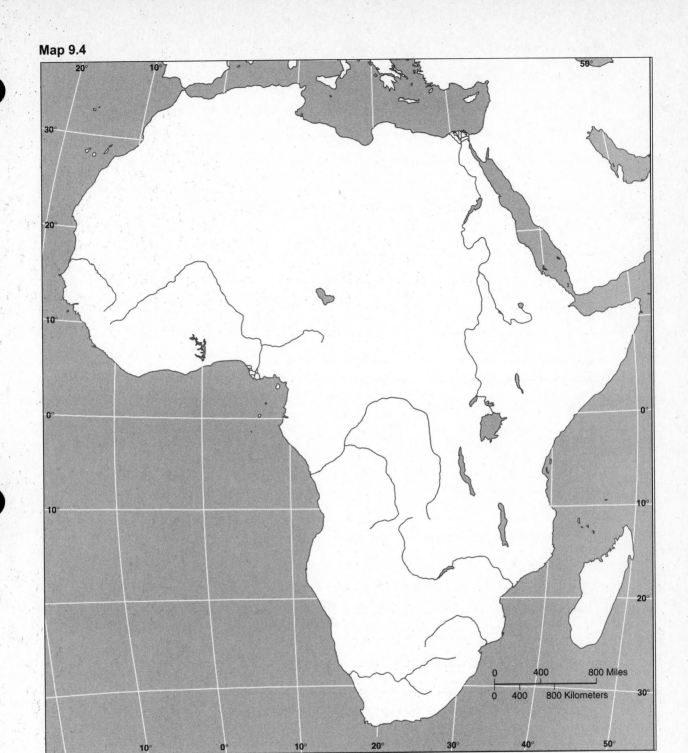